The Beautiful Evolving You

365 Days of Bliss

Brahmashakti Fudail

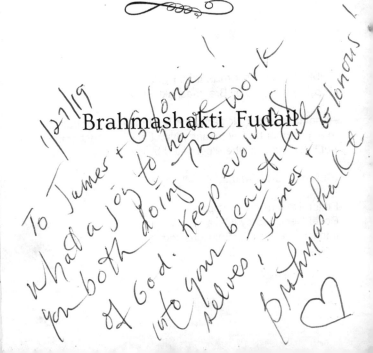

1/27/19

To James & Gloria!

What a joy to have work
you both doing. The glorious
of God. Keep evolving
into your beautiful / James &
selves! Brahmashakti

Published by Brahmashakti Fudail

ISBN: 978-0-692-41693-8

Editor: Dr. Maxine Thompson
Cover Designed by Ishwari
Interior Design: TWASolutions.com

Praises for
The Beautiful Evolving You: 365 Days of Bliss

"This is a great book to purchase. I would recommend that you buy it and see for yourself, that this book is a real gem."

–Benyamin Bridges, CEO: SES
(School of Entrepreneurial Skills)
Mt. Vernon, New York

"What a beautiful sharing with the humanity who is greatly in need. You are an inspiration. What is special about reading your book is I see you in the highest light, radiant and at Peace."

–Jayalakshmi Moss; Physical Therapist;
Student of Meditation and Yoga

"Truly inspiring daily devotional words. What a wonderful way to start the day!"

–Akua Ali Furlow , Educator and
Author of "The Tuskegee Syphilis
Study: What Really Happened"

"Insightful affirmations of the power of faith as applied to our daily life and tasks."

"This book is a road map to life. (It is)Perhaps the most important letter to God ever written. One has only to connect, meditate and write. God hears what is said and written. Dreams come true when you communicate with God."

DEDICATION

I dedicate this book of inspirational
Words and thoughts to God, who is my
Life and my Love.

ACKNOWLEDGMENTS

I would like to thank God and my spiritual teacher, Swamini Turiyasangitananda, for their guidance and love.

And to my husband, Chionesu, for his patience and listening ear while I read parts of the book to him deep into the midnight hour.

And to my sons who always prompted me along by saying, "Great job, Mom!"

I also would like to thank my editor, Dr. Maxine Thompson, for her keen eye and her professionalism. Love you, Sis!

Much love, respect and appreciation for my Ashram Family, who daily strive to keep God first and foremost in their lives. May you each continue to be a beacon of light, peace and love to all that you meet.

My sincere thank-you to my twin sister, Brahmachandri Bridges and fellow writer, Shankari Adams who both took the time out of their busy lives to read parts of the manuscript and offer very insightful comments and suggestions. Much love to you both.

Last but not least, I must give props to my writing group that I have been a proud member of since 2012; the Saturday Morning Literary Workshop in Los Angeles. I appreciate your expertise, constructive criticism, guidance and love that pushes me to keep on writing. Each of you are dynamite writers. I am proud to know you so intimately through your writings. All of you hold a very dear place in my heart. Thank you so much for being a part of my life.

PREFACE

I consider myself to have been used as an instrument; a co-writer with God and my spiritual teacher, Swamini Turiyasangitananda aka Alice Coltrane in the writing of this book. Often times, as I wrote these words, thoughts, feelings, tears of joy would come into my eyes. Whenever that happened, I knew deep down within, that particular thought for that day would resonate and uplift others as well. However, I must be honest! All the daily thoughts touched me deeply, and I hope that it will do the same for you.

During the writing of this book, I would often reflect back to when I was a pre-teen growing into teenage-hood during the early 1960's. I wished that I could have read simple affirmations like this. Not saying that I was not inspired by my mother, grandmother, relatives and dear friends, because I was. But I never read daily words of inspiration in a book for children my age back then to spike my interest to pursue meditation or silent sitting. Of course, I read the Bible, and fell in love with the Psalms, which helped me to feel and visualize peace and contentment. Also The Daily Word publication, introduced me to the great poet, James Dillet Freeman, who wrote frequently for The Daily Word. His positive affirmations began to open up my heart more and to want to go deeper within myself and find out who I truly was in God's Eyesight. By then, I was in my early twenties and had already started on my spiritual quest.

Today the pre-teens have tons of beautiful inspirational books with daily affirmations to help them deal with the daily challenges in life.

The Saturday Morning Literary Workshop writers group that I belong to in Los Angeles, and which I am currently Vice President, encouraged me immensely. I remember one Saturday when I had read a few inspiring thoughts from the book to the writers group. They became very quiet. My thoughts were, "Oh no, they don't like it. I am wasting my time." One 65 year old writer looked at me, and said, "Girl, this is not just for the young, this is for us old folks too. I love it. You got something very special."

I look forward to you reading my book, written for both the young and old. I pray that it will keep the fire going within you and help to burn out any negative energy; and replace it with positive thoughts of love for yourself, humanity and all of creation.

May these words within the book, inspire you to become The Beautiful Evolving You!

– *Brahmashakti Fudail*
Agoura, California
April 9, 2015

INTRODUCTION

As I read the selections for February, 9th, 10th, and 11th, I was reassured that the message of loving oneself rang out to me and that also inspired me to revisit my book in progress that includes affirmations. It seems as though Brahmashakti's work opened something deep in me that had closed up. A part of my own creativity was touched. Those few beautiful lines supercharged my initiative to complete and confirm my own connection with the perfect divine. What a gift your words are to all who hear.

Celebrate your magnificence with Brahmashakti, as you read and participate in this divine acknowledgement of the human spirit experience. I'm sure you'll be delighted!

I first met Brahmashakti and her family in the mid 90's. Brahmashakti and her family and her twin sister's family, are all from a wonderful dimension of goodness, spirituality, generosity, caring, love, wisdom, Godliness, transformation and devotion. It is with honor that I present a most magnificent life in the form of an author, teacher and inspirationalist. Brahmashakti has put her heart into fine motion here in *The Beautiful Evolving You: 365 Days of Bliss*. She encourages us to set daily intentions and affirmations for our being. She is healing and profound in sharing this offering. A new simple structure. A structure in which to organize our morning/evening devotional. A sacred ritual to creation itself. A unique collection of 365 power affirmations have been born.

Namaste,

Tico Wells, spiritual being and divine creative

January

January 1

I will start the New Year by walking through
The door to my inner self. I will not be
Frightened by what I see or feel. I will grow
Through my experiences and become the
Person that God needs me to be.

January 2

No matter what, I will try my best to
Give my all in every area of my
Life as I walk gently upon Mother Earth.

January 3

Learn to dance to the inner rhythm
Of your soul, that will propel
You forward to reach the ultimate
Goal of life:
GOD.

January 4

I think I can. I feel I can.
I know I can...
Help someone today.

January 5

I believe in the possible.
So I can do the impossible,
Just because I believe in God.
I am strong and stand tall
In my quest for Truth.
I will not fail.

January 6

I am drug-free and alcohol-free.
I soar high on God's Love.

January 7

I am full of positive vibrations
That connects me to everything
That is good, wholesome and beautiful.

January 8

Jesus said, "Knock and the door shall be
Opened." I open the door and walk the path,
Knowing that God is always with me.
My blessings are never-ending.

January 9

Jesus said, "Seek and Ye shall find."
By going within everyday to meditate,
I sit quietly and patiently to hear the answers
To all the questions that I ask.

January 10

Today I will step out in Faith and
Know that God is in control of my life.
I envision a fantastic day filled with
Love, creativity and awareness.
I am ready to share with all.

January 11

I can conquer all enemies by
Surrounding myself with Love.
For God is Love and
Love triumphs over all.

January 12

I am a truth seeker for the highest good.
I surround myself in Truth while
Living on sweet Mother Earth.
I know that I am well protected
Because my Father told me so.

January 13

I will start this day off by taking control of my
Life. After my day is complete, I will
Then surrender it back to God.

January 14

Writing your ideas down is a
Good start for those who
Listen and act upon their ideas.
Believe in what you want,
And feel and see.
As long as your ideas have meaning
And a positive purpose,
Then do it, feel it, live it.

January 15

I keep a smile on my face,
Even when the going gets rough.
I stick it out to the end.
I then become the victor.

January 16

Even when my body is down,
I lift mine eyes up to the Lord.
He is my Doctor; Physician, prescribing
The perfect medicine for my cure.

January 17

When the troubles of this world become too
Much, I run for safety into the Sanctuary of
My heart. I sit in silence. I pray until I am
At Peace again. Then I return back to the
World—strengthened and refreshed.

January 18

I love to help others.
I love to make people happy,
Because what goes around,
Comes around… guaranteed!

January 19

I will help my friends
By being there for them when needed.
I will say a prayer for them; hold counsel
With them, if they wish.
I will let them know that I care.
That is what friends are for.

January 20

I opened up my mind and saw
The impossible become a reality right
Before my eyes because of
My faith and trust in God.

January 21

Today I will let go of all the negative thoughts.
I will embrace all the positive thoughts
That will bring me closer to God.

January 22

With God, I am large and
In charge of Our life together.
He is my Guide and my Savior.
I just love the Lord.

January 23

God is in everything I do;
Every little thing I do is for God.
I cannot fail, because He is
My Guiding Light, always.

January 24

I can only do the right thing when
My thoughts are on The Most High.
I get uplifted and inspired to
Become the winner that I know I am.
God is always in my corner.
How can I fail?

January 25

To know God
Is on my list of "Things to Do."
It is the number one priority in my life.
It gives me the get up and don't quit attitude
That makes me feel good about me and
My aspiring relationship with the Lord.

January 26

If we would wear beautiful
Thoughts as we do clothing;
Together we could become seekers
Of truth and wisdom.
We would then celebrate the
Union of the soul and self,
As One.

January 27

Live right,
Do right,
Think right,
Talk right,
Walk correctly on the path of Life.
You will become a blessing
To all that you meet.

January 28

The greatest offering that we
Can give to God is to serve and love our
Fellow brothers and sisters who are in need.
Together, in unity, we would create
A world of radiant Light-Workers.

January 29

I promise to love God and to please God
In everything that I do, say and think.
I ask God to please help me be successful
To confront the challenges head on;
Eventually wearing the
Banner of success across my chest

January 30

Dear God. Please help me
To always stay true to whom I am.
For You and I are one:
One Love;
One Life;
One Truth.

January 31

The "I" is now a "We". We are one, forever...
We cannot leave each other, never.
God is around me and guides me.
I am beside Him and I walk with Him.
It is true inter-connectedness,
We are connected as one in divine love....

February

February 1

Every morning is the first day of my life.
I will always try to wake up, empowered with
Strength, love and compassion.

February 2

Do you hear the birds singing
Early in the morning?
This is Nature's way of getting
Us up to rejoice and be happy.
I, too, will sing my song of joy
To God early in the morning.

February 3

I will never give up. I will always move
Forward and try my best to be successful
In everything that I do, think and say.

February 4

When I cry, may it be for others and
Not for my own selfish needs and wants.

February 5

Let me be a blessing to all that I meet.
May I selflessly shed some light of Hope
And peace for others on my way to God.

February 6

May my dance on Mother Earth always
Be meaningful and full of the correct turns,
Dips and steps that are pleasing to the Lord.

February 7

Today I wake up to a brand new me.
I am renewed and fortified by a good
Night's sleep, ready to take on the world,
By saying my prayers in the morning.
I am a better and a more loving me,
Ready to serve God.

February 8

There is so much I want to do in life.
So I write a plan to follow, and,
If needed, change a plan, and
Then offer it to God.
Success is sure to follow.

February 9

Today I release the chains that bind me
And walk in the awareness of the great I Am.

February 10

Believe in yourself...
Appreciate yourself...
Humble yourself...
Declare yourself to be
A fountain of love, peace and
Light for all to see.
Be about goodness and make
Your life an example of what it
Feels like and looks like to love the Lord.

February 11

Love yourself. Love yourself. Love yourself...
Don't be afraid to love yourself into
Wholeness and completeness.
Pass it on....

February 12

Jump into life with a high exuberance to serve
God.
Now play the game of life to win.

February 13

When I pray for others, I
Get down on my knees and
Pour my heart out to God:
"Lord, please shine Your effulgent
Light of mercy and compassion
Down upon us, to heal and renew us.
Shower us with Your sweet nectar,
Recharge our light with your love,
Beloved God, so we can do Your work
And reach the mountain top."
Amen.

February 14

You have so much to give....
Dig deep down inside and always give
Your utmost best to everything
That you do for God.

February 15

Love God. Love your friends.
Love your family. Pray for your
Enemies to overcome their anger.
Find a happy medium and indulge
Yourself in God-filled thoughts.

February 16

Freedom. I have
Freedom to be at ease with myself.
Freedom to be at one with God.
Freedom to go deep within to
Make the right choices.
Freedom to be victorious.

February 17

I am so grateful to God for
All He has done for me.
Thank You…
Thank You…
Thank You…

February 18

Being able to help others
In need is very important.
It is a blessing for everyone
Involved. The outcome results in
A loving and win-win
Situation for all.

February 19

Love the person you are.
Strive to be the very best that you can be.
That is the greatest gift you can give
Yourself, in the form of
Love and service to others.

February 20

I pray that I can accept all the daily
Happenings in my life, with gratitude and
Thankfulness. I pray that I can see the good,
Even in what I consider a "messy" situation
And come out on top of life's game.

February 21

Laughter is one of the best medicines
To help give more balance and joy to life.
So laugh and feel whole and beautiful every
Day. Share your laughter with someone
And pass it on.

February 22

I have a life to live.
I choose to live it in service to others.
Over and over… Again and again…
In peace and with Love.

February 23

I love me. I love everything about me.
And if there is something about me that
I do not like, I have the power to change it.
I do this fearlessly and without self-judgment.

February 24

All power to God the Most High.
Thank You God for being so wonderful,
So caring and so kind.
All praises to the Almighty God.

February 25

Be true and loving to yourself.
Be kind and patient to yourself.
Be intelligent and meditative.
Your light will shine brightly on
The path to God so others may
follow Your lead.

February 26

Today is a good day.
Today is a great day to rejoice in
The name of the Lord.
Today I will claim my oneness with
The Most High. Come and join me as
We claim our divine birth right in God.

February 27

I will always pray to live a life for God.
I am able to do that because God
Always answers the sincere prayer.
I thank you, God.

February 28

Get up and feel good about yourself every day.
Prove to yourself what God already knows....
How truly fantastic you really are!

February 29

It is okay if you are not considered hip or cool
By your peers. Help to create a world that
Celebrates and acknowledges people for
Who they are, and the good that they
Bring to the table.

March

March 1

Prepare yourself for a wonderful life in God.
Be ready to sit in silence when you meditate
With the Lord so you can hear His divine
Guidance. Leave there feeling exuberant and
Ready to inspire others.

March 2

Be strong.
Believe in yourself.
Do your duty to God and
Your country.
Be proud of who you are.
Be happy when
You are helping others.
Where ever you live, be ready
To serve the Lord
By providing service to others.

March 3

If you believe and have faith in God,
Then everywhere you look, you will see the
Glory of the Most High in the daily activities
In your life, for God will not hide from you.

March 4

I believe in myself,
I believe in you,
I believe in
God.

March 5

Let us show love for all of our brothers
And sisters in the world. Then wars will
Be a thing of the past. Love will prevail.

March 6

Be a voice for those whose voices
Are not being heard. Step up a notch
Or two, and help create one united
Voice of humanity under God.

March 7

All creation should be in harmony with
Its Maker. I will help to build a peaceful
Kingdom of God While on Mother Earth.

March 8

Less is better.
Less ego.
Less false pride.
Less fighting.
Less hatred.
We should work on chipping away at
This mountain of ignorance daily.
Results: A more humble human being.
A better and loving world.

March 9

Today, let us all gather our vocal instruments;
And, as one voice, harmoniously
Sing about our oneness with God.

March 10

Look for words of wisdom
From unexpected persons
In surprising places, like the
Laundry-mat; movie theater or a
Football stadium. One never knows
What words of wisdom folks
May speak to you;
Just short of amazing,
That will make you grow and
Become a better person.

March 11

Help me, God, to see the good in
Everyone, as You do.
Let us see without judgment
And without fear,
But with Love and
Respect for one another,
Like You do.
Amen

March 12

Each country has an official language that
Each individual of that particular country
Speaks. However, Love is the official language
Of God. Wherever you are today, spread
Happiness. Speak God's language—Love.

March 13

"Surely all the days of my life I shall dwell in
the House of the Lord, forever and forever.
Amen." Thank you, God.

March 14

Take care of your self. Keep your body clean.
Keep your thoughts clean. Go forward in God.

March 15

Live simple, so others can just simply live.

March 16

Be aware of how you move on Mother Earth.
Listen to "The Inner Drummer."
Make the right moves. You will be successful.

March 17

When you find your true love
To walk the path of life with you,
Remember to always honor and
Respect that person.

March 18

Take it easy…Breathe slowly… Go deep and
Begin to explore the inner you. Your heart
Will expand. You will radiate Love.
Love = God
God = Love

March 19

I am not afraid to begin to look within and
Unwrap the package that is marked fragile…
That package which is me.

March 20

Each day I rekindle my own love for myself.
I sit in quietness in the sanctuary of my heart
And introspect on who I am. I find myself
More in Love with myself and whom I
represent: God....

March 21

At times, I am in awe and wonderment.
Sometimes I am confused and angry.
I turn to my Lord to help me become
Centered. I can experience peace again.

March 22

I ask God to help me through the maze
Of the many me's that I portray. I need
To find the loving God personality
That fits me best,
And to wear it as my banner of Truth.
I know my Lord will help me.
As always, I give thanks.

March 23

Through introspection, I find that it is
Okay to react differently to the various
Dramas in my life. I know that I must work
On being calm in all situations and
Being non-judgmental.
I must let Truth be my guide.

March 24

God is my Best Friend.
When I fall down, my Best Friend
Always has my back.
And that is a fact.

March 25

Love, Love, Love…
Let's say that a little louder;
LOVE, LOVE, LOVE,
Just a little louder now.
Everyone shout,
"LOVE!"

March 26

I believe in Magic.
God is Magic.
Magnificent,
Majestic,
Sublime Magic.
God takes all the guess work
Out of the problem and
Reveals the solution.
I will walk the path with my
Magician at all times.

March 27

Good Morning, God! I will let your
Sweetness permeate in everything
That I do this day....My day is
Filled with love and gratitude,
Just because of You.

March 28

God and I are one.
Me and the God Force are united.
The Most High Supreme One and I
Are in total commitment to each other.
Now that is very, very cool.

March 29

Every day, let God hear your endearments
To Him. Your endearments to God fuel your
Vehicle of existence on the spiritual path.
He will protect and guide you always.

March 30

Stay young at heart;
Listen to good music;
Speak gently, sweetly and softly;
Honor your parents.
Serve others in need, and
God will fill your life with good
Health and prosperity.

March 31

All we need is Love…
All we need is Peace…
All we need is Non-Violence…
All we need is Truth…
All we need is Right Conduct…
All will lead you to God,
Whom we all need.

April

April 1

Begin to write about your spiritual journey.
Write about your spiritual encounters and
Introspect on them daily. By the end of the
Year, you will see how far you have
Progressed on the path back to God.

April 2

I love who I am.
I am a fabulous person.
I feel the infinite sweetness of
God's love and protection around me.
I am truly blessed!

April 3

Walk around with an attitude of gratitude.
You will permeate your environment with
Appreciation. You will encourage those around
You to think more Positive thoughts and want
To live in peace with one another.

April 4

Don't allow the mind to dwell on negative
Thoughts. You are in charge of what you
Think! Switch to thoughts that allow beauty
To take over and prevail your mind.

April 5

Today, I will stand in my integrity.
I will be honest in thought, word and deed.
I will build my identity on the words
That I speak and the actions I perform.
I only attract good.

April 6

I AM a lover of all things good. I instill all
Good things within me. I live my life wisely
And with respect to all living beings. I AM.

April 7

Blessings to all that I meet and greet today.
As I walk my walk today, I will take
Special note of what it is that makes me
Smile and fills me up with love.
At the end of the day, I realize that the
"WOW" factor is none other than
GOD.

April 8

Here we are, living on sweet Mother Earth.
Living, laughing, loving, serving, giving
And receiving. How blessed we are to
Know our purpose in life, which is to love
And to serve God.

April 9

Lord, I pray to be
A Light Worker...
A Positive Word Maker...
A Peace Maker...
A Soldier in God's Army
Stay in-love-all
The-Time-With-God-Lover.
Amen

April 10

Cry out to the Lord, from
The depths of your soul,
When you are in a dark place.
Surely, He will come to you,
When you repeatedly call
His Name in earnest.
Quickly, He has arrived to
Soothe your troubled heart.

April 11

During the waking hours,
Keep God on your mind.
Wherever you are and whomever you
Are with; whatever you are doing,
Keep God first.

April 12

Practice repeating the
Lord's name silently within.
By continuously repeating
His name, it will turn into sugary
Musical notes, constantly playing
In the back of your mind.
Propelling you forward on
The path to God...
To freedom....

April 13

Let the name of God forever
Be upon your lips, in holy praise,
Love and worship.
Whether praising Him silently
Or out loud, rejoice in celebrating
The Holy names of God daily.

April 14

Prayers are when you are
Talking to God and
Asking Him questions.
Meditation is when you sit
Quietly, waiting for the answers.
"Wait, I say on the Lord."

April 15

Whenever that great feeling of
Love wells up inside of you,
Consciously move that joyous
Feeling all through your body,
Letting it simmer and take
Control of you. Relax.
You are now ready to meditate.

April 16

Keep your thoughts on God,
As much as possible.
You will feel better.
You will think better.
You will act better,
You will speak softer
And sweeter.
Plus, look super-fantastic!

April 17

In the still of the early
Morning, arise. Talk to God. Tell Him
Your concerns, your joys and your sorrows.
Listen carefully in meditation for the answers
And directions. "Be still and know that
I am God."

April 18

Be strong. Don't let other
People persuade you to do
Something that you know deep
Down inside of you is wrong.
Live according to the laws of God.
You will realize that living a life
For God is never boring,
But filled with endless joy
And divine adventure.

April 19

Stay positive and keep God in
The forefront of your mind.
That way, Dr. Evil will
Find another 'house' to reside in.
For it can never live in a
Heart that is filled
With the love of God.
Open up the windows of your
Soul and let the Light shine within
Your place of worship.

April 20

God and you are one.
Imagine that you played
Together and were best friends
And were inseparable when younger.
You are now older and realize this Truth.
Know that He will always love you.
Thank God for keeping you then, now
And always…

April 21

Develop a burning desire to
Stay in God's Grace. For His
Grace is a healing balm that
Will instantly soothe and calm
You in the face of any storm.
Be strong
Stay strong…
Put your trust in God.

April 22

The Inner Drummer lives
In each of us.
Listen well and move to
That powerful and righteous
Drum beat.
Allow the Inner Drummer and
Your heart to become one
Synchronized beat, offering
Melodious sounds of love
To the Most High.

April 23

When you open your eyes, feeling
Grumpy and out of sorts,
Just lie there and
Call on the Lord for help.
When you are centered again,
Get up, stand strong with your feet
On the floor, hug yourself and ask,
"God, how may I serve you today?"

April 24

The Master has a creative
Plan just for you.
How will you know?
Because you will feel anxious,
Happy and sad, all at the
Same time. You will burn with a

Desire to want to serve God.
Go to that sweet seat of meditation
Within your private sanctuary;
Your heart.
Be still.
Wait on the Lord.
Merge with Him.

April 25

Listen. Go deeper.
Listen more. Go deeper still.
Sit with pen and paper
By your side, ready to write
Down His creative plan that
He has designed just
For you to carry out.

April 26

God's creative plan of action this lifetime
Should be carried out in
Devotion and Selflessness.
God will never leave
You on your own.
Call on Him whenever you
Need to overcome the problems
That are blocking you from
Carrying out His plan.
His love for you will clear the path
And lead you to victory.

April 27

You will receive so
Much joy on the
Journey to God.
When you let go of the pain
You encounter in life,

You are also allowing others
To let go of their pain.
When you love yourself,
You allow others to love themselves.

April 28

Blossom without guilt.
Be who you truly are,
Without guilt.
Help others, serve others,
Be kind to others,
Without guilt.
Nurture yourself;
Love yourself,
Without guilt.

April 29

May waves of peace,
Waves of love,
Waves of joy, and
Waves of gratitude
Genuinely wrap
Itself around your life, always…

April 30

Move forward unafraid.
Move forward in strength.
Move forward in serenity.
Move forward in worship.
Begin and continue to
Move forward with
The Lord, our God.

May

May 1

Be gracious to others.
Be polite and courteous to all.
For how you treat others,
Is how you will be treated.
Remember:
"What goes around comes around."

May 2

Respect the:
Four-legged,
Creepy crawlers,
The winged ones
And all water beings
On sacred Mother Earth.
For they too have a part
To play in this
Drama called Life.

May 3

Focus on integrity.
Practice telling the truth,
Even when it may
Get you in trouble.
For one lie can lead to another,
Until you have built a mountain
Of lies. Then what?
People may not believe
Or trust you anymore.
You may lose good friends.
So speak the truth always,
Even when it may be unpopular.
You will be respected for
Having the strength to stand tall,
With integrity.

May 4

Choose your friends carefully.
True friends will tell you the
Truth, to your face and not
Behind your back.
They will be there for you,
In the good times
And in the sad times.
They will have your back.

May 5

When an unpleasant thought
Comes to mind, get rid of it.
By simply thinking of
Something beautiful,
You will feel better.
It is that easy!

May 6

Think better of yourselves!
That's right.
Young men, keep your pants up!
Young ladies, don't show
So much skin.
Respect yourselves and
Be a shining example to the
Younger ones, who look
Up to you in admiration.

May 7

When I fill myself
Up with God's Love,
It shows in my eyes,
The way I walk,
The way I talk,
The way I carry myself.
God is written all over me.
I am protected for life.

May 8

Pay it forward in
Service to people.
Be a voice for one
Who is afraid or shy;
Pay it forward
To help those in need
Who cannot find their own voice.

May 9

When you are feeling down,
Just wrap your warm, loving
Arms around yourself.
Tell yourself that
Everything is going to be okay.
Believe it. Feel it.
Have hope and faith and
Know that God will
Pull you through.

May 10

Dance! Dance! Dance!
Sing! Sing! Sing!
Jump! Jump! Jump!
In the privacy of your space,
Yell! Scream! Shout
Out God's names.
Feeling real good yet?
Now go out and
Make an amazing difference
In the world.

May 11

I can do this;
I can be this;
I can build this;
I can believe this;
I can visualize this;

I can create what I need,
To elevate myself and others
On the spiritual path.
For I am an extraordinary
Person working for the Lord.
All the goodness and sweetness of life in God.

May 12

I strive to do the right thing
Every day.
I begin to see
The love and protection of
God surrounding me.
He fulfills my wishes in ways
That I didn't think were possible.

May 13

I am who I am.
I sit quietly every day
To find out a little more
About me and my role here.
I change a little bit
Every day, by sitting
Quietly and listening to
The Voice within.
I like who I am becoming.

May 14

I fold my hands together
When I say my prayers.
I fold my hands in prayer
When I get down on
My knees and talk to God.
I fold my hands in prayer
And cry tears of joy when
God talks to me.
I am loved.

May 15

Everywhere you look,
You will see God,
If your heart is open
And receptive to His Love.
For I worship God,
And God knows that
I always will.

May 16

If I can't look at
My problem,
I won't be able to
Fix the problem.
I will face the problem,
So I can fix the problem.

May 17

You are building and creating
What you want, like an architect.
With unlimited thoughts,
You can create what you need.
Create all the good you
Want in your life.
Work with the
Divine Architect:
God.

May 18

Every day, try to remove all doubts
And worries from your mind.
It may be a long process,
But go forward in faith and
Know that the
Best is yet to come.

May 19

Walk in harmony.
Work in harmony.
Live in harmony
With each other and nature.

May 20

Live your life in enjoyment.
Live your life in merriment.
Live your life in love.
Live your life with intelligence.
Play the game of life to win.

May 21

Don't be afraid to step
Into your power,
Into your light.
You are a strong person.
Start now to recognize
Who you truly are.
Don't be afraid.

May 22

Smile, laugh, live,
Love and focus.
Surrender to God.
Keep on smiling, laughing
Living, loving and focusing;
Surrendering to God.

May 23

Prepare yourself to be
Who you want to be.
Be what you want to be.
Be the real you.
Experience the real you.
Be in love with the real you.
Now rejoice and
Live in peace.

May 24

When the weary blues of this
Mundane world leaves me feeling
Down and out, I cry out
To God from the depths of my
Heart to come and stand with me;
To make me strong again.
He arrives quickly to restore me
Back to happy and faithful; for
The Lord answers all sincere prayers.

May 25

God is Love
Love is God.
Don't become
Engulfed in an illusion,
Believing that God
Is not what He is.
For God is all that,
And so very much more.
Inwardly, you already know that!

May 26

I received my report card today from God.
He gave me 4 A's; 2 B's and 1 Must Do.
My heart dropped when I saw the Must Do!
What did He mean? Where did I go wrong?
I thought I was giving Him my all.
I smiled when I saw what He wrote.

"My dear," God wrote.
"You must now meditate
Longer on Me, so the Kingdom of Heaven is
yours.
I will now give you more bliss in your
meditations,
So that way you will meditate deeper and
reach your
Journey's end in Me."
I laughed. I cried. I was ecstatic with joy.
What a wonderful life I have.

May 27

The easiest thing to do
To make our lives very
Simple and lovely, is to
Just surrender everything
To God.
Therefore, we

Know that God's infinite
Protection and guidance
Will always be ours.

May 28

You are my Inhale;
You are my Exhale;
You are my Everything.
I breathe in your Love, your
Happiness, your
Sweet Fragrance.
I am your vivid and living
Expression of Love.
Yes, God, my Love,
I am in you.
You are in me.

May 29

You are in love!
You can't hide it!
I can tell by the way
You walk, as if on air.
Your eyes are shining;
You look happier, and
Speak more eloquently.
You are more kindhearted.
I see you! I see you!
You have finally fallen in love.
With God.

May 30

We are one with each other,
No matter how we, as humanity, see
Ourselves in this big picture called life.
In order to figure out how

And why we fit in;
We must sit quietly; meditate.
This will help us
To stay on
The right path
To self-discovery.

May 31

Have confidence in who you are.
Love yourself thoroughly.
Look deep within yourself
At your own flaws.
Work on getting rid of them.
By correcting your own imperfections,
You will be less inclined to correct
And judge others.

June

June 1

Everybody has the ability
To be great because
Everyone has the ability
To serve others.
When you serve others, you
Stand out and brilliantly
Shine in the eyes of the Lord.

June 2

What it was, was Love;
What it is, is Love;
What it is to be and
Forever more is Love.
Love is God.

June 3

Let the feeling of
Happiness continue to
Grow and grow
Until it explodes
Into more seeds of
Happiness spreading everywhere.
Stay in your center of bliss
Which will help to wipe away tears
And bring enjoyment to others.

June 4

You are filled with
The excellent and positive
Ingredients needed to live
A righteous life in God.
Abundant and a joy-filled
Life is yours, as long as
You believe in God.
Stay cheerful.

June 5

Don't be a bystander
In your own life.
Don't wait for someone
Else to lay out plans
For your own life.
Meditate and pray to God.
He will show you your life's purpose
And how to accomplish it.
Give thanks for all of
The help given to you from Him.

June 6

I am here to change
The world.
Watch out! Here I come in
The forms of
Peace, love and joy.
Here I am…

Here I will always be…
Loving myself and
Serving God.

June 7

Something is taking over
My walk, my talk,
My thoughts, my body.
A wonderful feeling is
Taking over me.
This feeling is lovingly
Inviting me to step out in faith;
To take the plunge into the
Never-ending me.
Don't be afraid. Find out
Who you are.
God will guide you through
Your spiritual journey, for
He is with you, always….

June 8

Don't play yourself small.
Don't be afraid to live
In your greatness.
Be great if you dare,
For that is who you
Truly are;
A grand individual who is
Of the light and of love.
Dare to be you....

June 9

You are a magnificent,
Walking and living
Embodiment of love,
Amazement, joy and light.
You have got to be you.
Because no one else
Can play your role of
Being you. Except you!
Step up. Step out.

June 10

Love is the greatest
Truth on the planet.
To know this truth and
To live in this truth,
Will free you of pain,
And allow you to live
In harmony.

June 11

A Lighthouse helps to guide
People and boats away from
Dangerous rocks.
Be like a Lighthouse.
Be a gift of light that glows
With happiness and confidence
So others can be influenced by
Your shining example.

June 12

When you have integrity,
You do not settle for just anything;
You settle only for the best
Of everything.
For you are worth it.

June 13

Don't compare yourself
To others. It can bring
On despair and tears.
Everybody has his or her
Unique gifts to offer.
Some gifts are shared early
On in life. Other gifts unwrap
In a particular season.
All gifts are opened
When they are ready.

June 14

Own up to the artist within you.
You are the creative expression
Of all that is.
The list is never-ending.
Let it be revealed to you
Through meditation that you
Are part of the great I Am.

June 15

Come with me to the
Land of the enjoyable
And appreciative people.
There you will bask in
The knowingness of what
Defines 'happy'.
Happy is loving who
You are… And
Being grateful to
The Happy Source.
God.

June 16

Before you accuse,
Argue or judge someone,
Ask yourself, "What part
Have I played in this situation?"
Meditate and go
Deep within yourself.
God will provide the
Perfect solution.

June 17

Who you are right now,
Guarantees that you will not be the
Same person in the next
Minute, hour or day.
You will grow and
Keep adding on to who you are,
Day by day…
Year by year…
Get ready to blossom into an
Extra-ordinary person.

June 18

As a young person, it
Can be hard to stay in
The moment and remain
Focused.
But this is a constant
Lesson that you will
Have to practice daily.
For when you are in
The moment, you are truly
Connected to those around you.

June 19

In order to help others,
You must have
Peace in your heart.
Then you can lend a helping
Hand to those in need.
They will feel your
Peace and love,
And be calm.

June 20

Bring a smile to
Someone's face.
Be happy. Be nice.
Extend a helping hand.
Treat others the way
You want to be treated.
We will have a better world
Because of your kindness.

June 21

Your happiness should
Not depend on someone else.
Go to the Source for happiness.
Go to the Source for guidance.
Go to the Source for Love.
Go to the Source for everything!
We all know who
The true Source is
God…

June 22

I wake up feeling
Your love, Lord.
I place my attention on You,
Awaiting your command.
I will be of service today.
I am prepared, strong and
God-filled this day
To do Your work.

June 23

He is Beautiful.
He is Self-less.
He is Strong and Powerful.
He is God...
My Knight in Shining Armor.

June 24

I will strive to do my best every day.
When I fall down, I will get up.
I will keep going because
I am made up of God-stuff.
Good stuff. Strong stuff,
That will get up, fight the devil
And be victorious.
Good stuff that lives in God.

June 25

Honor yourself, so you
May honor others.
Respect yourself, so you
May respect others.
Love yourself, so you
May love others....
This is the path to
God-Realization.

June 26

Are you in tune
With whom you are?
Do you know how to
Give yourself a tune-up?
When you are out of tune,
You are not your happy self.
Here's a suggestion:
Find a quiet place,
Sit down, close your eyes.
Breath deep. Relax.
Let go…let go…
Let God
Fill you back up
Again, empowered in love.

June 27

You are beautiful, show it.
You are wonderful, express it.
You are creative, make it.
You are original, bask in it.
You are love, express it in
Its many marvelous ways.

June 28

There are many paths
that lead to God.
God who allows us
To have choices also allows
Us to choose Him or not.
You have to decide. But
By beholding His Magnificence,
The unanimous choice
By most is that they choose God.

June 29

The Source, The Pipeline,
Of our being is the one
Incredible God, who shadows us,
Always…
How fortunate we are
To have such a
Magnificent Friend.

June 30

God is All-Hearing;
God is All-Knowing;
God is All-Seeing.
And He is all ours
To love and to treasure.

July

July 1

The Heart-Beat of our being
Is the Sweet One. He is the one magnificent
God, who is with us always.
He sees everything.
He is Omnipresent;
He is the All-Seeing One.

July 2

The Wisest Magician of all times,
Helps to create situations for us to learn
And grow from. He is an Awesome God,
Who needs us to remember who we truly are.
Hence, the growing pains. Therefore,
He waits patiently for the day that we will
Wake up and realize our oneness with Him.
He is Omniscient;
The All-Knowing One.

July 3

The Supreme Spiritual Warrior in our lives
Is the Great One, who
Is with us always, shielding and
Protecting us from harm.
He is Omnipotent;
The All-Powerful One:
The Lord Supreme.

July 4

Don't be afraid to show happiness.
It is okay for you to be filled with
Joy and to express it in a smile.
So, let the corners of your mouth curl
Up and form that beautiful smile!
Your smile may very well help to save
Someone from doing something terrible.
Smiling can be contagious.

July 5

God is my best friend ever.
When my other friends
Let me down, God is
Always there for me.
Patiently, He waits for
Me. He enfolds me in Love;
Letting me know that
Everything will be alright.

July 6

Keep God in your heart.
Your heart is your sanctuary,
Your church, your quiet space,
Reserved only for you.
No one else.
Go there; rest and speak to
God when it is too noisy outside.

July 7

Be happy for your friends when
Wonderful things happen for them
And change their lives forever.
You are sharing in their joy;
A sign of true friendship.

July 8

Practice good habits.
One great habit to work on
Is self-control.
Once you have mastered
self-control, you really
have everything.
It is freedom!

July 9

Speak with the elders.
The senior citizens
Will answer your
Questions about life, and the way it was.
They will guide you and help make your
Walk on Earth easier and more
Accessible to all
The joy and mercy that is
Given from God.

July 10

Key ingredients to living a good life:
Love God; Love yourself;
Follow God's Laws;
Respect yourself and others;
Honor your mother and father;
Have no fear;
Be strong;
Be loving;
Be yourself.

July 11

Be humble…
Stay open and receptive
To the many teachings
Presented to you daily
From people and
Life's experiences.
You will evolve into
A more compassionate person.

July 12

God is the Almighty One;
He is one without a second;
He is my glorious sunrise and my
Beautiful sunset;
God is everything.
He is the true love you
Are searching for.
Stop and listen; for He
Abides in your heart.

July 13

Keep praying. I daily make prayers
An important part of my life.
Prayers have removed the biggest
Obstacles from my path because
I have absolute
Faith that God is the Do-er!

July 14

Express your kindness,
Graciousness and helpful attitude
To others. Be an example to your
Friends, so they too will
Take steps towards being
Generous, friendly and righteous.

July 15

I will decide to be happy
Always…
Yes, I know it will be a
Challenge, but I will work on it;
Make it a priority.
For when I am happy,
God is happy.
And that is a beautiful feeling.

July 16

God is the Author of my life,
Who writes sweet words of love
In the tabernacle of my heart.
I love Him so much. He is my
Soul mate; the Light in my eyes.
I need God. And that is the truth.

July 17

Be grateful.
Stay humble.
Being a good listener
Leads to greater awareness.
It will bring
You to the Truth.
Thus, making you
A person of integrity
And honesty.

July 18

I must believe that I do
Have a wonderful life.
I must value my life and know
That I do live in peace and love.

July 19

Whatever names you
Call God, whether it be:
Jesus, Allah, Krishna
Or Jehovah,
In your time of need,
When you call upon Him
With a sincere heart, He will
Arrive quickly at your side.

July 20

Love is everywhere.
I have love in my heart.
I have love in my home
I love my parents; my family.
I love my friends.
I talk softly
And sweetly.
I walk in love…
I am love.

July 21

I thank you, God
I acknowledge you, God
For being the driving
Force in my life.
I thank you, God,
For all that you do
For me.
Yes, indeed.

July 22

I will end the struggle of
Trying to be like her or him.
I am who I am.
I am love, light and bliss!
I dance in joy and know
That I am a truth seeker
A lover of God.

July 23

Meditation helps me to become
Focused and balanced. It helps
Me to get in touch with my
Higher self, which will lead to
Communication with the Source.

July 24

I will help to create a positive
And rippling effect of
Love and harmony.
I am centered in love.
I am a beacon of light
To all that I meet.

July 25

I will let my positive words and
Selfless actions echo
With whom I truly am.
I am a person of light and love.
I am a soldier in God's Army.

July 26

Breathe life and energy into your life's work.
Make it come alive to build
A foundation of truth and awareness
That will help to open up people's hearts,
Allowing feelings of love and harmony to flow.
They will testify that unity
Among humanity can last a life time.

July 27

Go deep within and connect
To the Lord of everything.
Breathe out all unsacred thoughts.
Infuse your body with the glorious
Dawn of Light;
Bathing you anew.

July 28

I won't allow Jealousy,
Greed and Anger to raise their
Ugly heads and get
The best of me.
I will get rid of them by
Staying in a place of love.
Love conquers all.
Love will escort them
Out of my life.

July 29

God, you are my everything;
You are my all;
You are my adjectives; my verbs;
My plurals; my nouns;
You created it all!
I can talk about your
Good and holy gifts
That you give us
All day long.
You are…
Yes, you are
God.

July 30

Once I obtain the
Deep Love of the Lord,
That is all I will ever need.
His Love is so powerful,
I will strive to keep
His Love forever in
My heart.

July 31

I will strive to develop
Awesome virtues like being:
Charitable,
Giving,
Thankful,
Forgiving,
Fearless.
These virtues will bring
Me to the Feet of the Lord.

August

August 1

I didn't always believe in myself,
But I do now.
I didn't honor myself, but I do now.
I disliked me once, but I love myself now.
Therefore, I am straight
Forward in what I say.
I will speak from my heart.
I will speak the Truth.

August 2

I will not let the green grass fool me.
I will stay away from drugs and
Anything that is harmful to my
Body and mind that will
Keep me from my Lord.
For once I got in touch with
My higher self, I continuously
Introspected to make sure I was
Always about the business of God.

I receive subtle constant reminders
From the universe and nature to stay the course;
The course outlined by God.

August 3

Thank you…Thank you…Thank you…
A little bit louder now.
Thank you…Thank you…Thank you, God!
For all that You do for me.

August 4

There are many races,
Many religions and
Billions of people
On Mother Earth.
Each one is dancing his
Way back to God;
Including you and me.

August 5

Please help me God to make the
Right decisions as I strive to accomplish my
Divine purpose on Mother Earth.

August 6

The only fear one should have is that
Of being ignored by God.
God has His listening Ears
Attuned to you and me always…
I will try my very best
To think, to speak and to act
According to His Supreme
Laws and make Him
Number one in my life.

August 7

Love yourself.
Be kind to yourself and others as
You make your way back home to the Truth…
The journey to God will be
Difficult at times.
However, blaze your path
With faith and hope
And keep moving forward.

August 8

God's Light is brighter
Than all the lights in
The universe.
God's Light will save me
And encourage me to
Always stay focused on
Him…
forever….

August 9

I will live a full
Life in God.
The naysayers will not
Sway me off the
Path of light.
I walk in love, filled
With strength, power
And creativity.
Let us all say, "Amen!"

August 10

When you fail to get
The results you want,
Don't give up!
Renew your determination,
And keep at it.
Success will certainly follow.

August 11

I am a Light Being; so are you.
I am a Love Being; so are you.
We help our family and
Friends by speaking
Kindly, and respecting
Each other every day.

August 12

I am free to be the greatest
Person that I can be.
That is my choice.
So I will continue to make
Good choices in my life
To bring out my very best,
That will shine the light on
My path to Joy.

August 13

Love is everywhere…
Love is in our hearts…
Love is in our homes…
Love is universal…
Love is in me…
Love is in you…
So let the waves of joy and love
Reverberate throughout the world.

August 14

When you have to make a
Decision, do so.
Think it through and then decide.
For if you don't, life will make the decision
For you which you may not like.
Unsolved, it will nag you until
You come up with a solution.
Some resolution is
Better than none.

August 15

I am me…
I am a confident me…
I am a brilliant me…
I am a gifted me…
I am a caring me…
All of this equals a
Very unique
Me.

August 16

God's work is never ending.
I work with God by
Helping others, so, therefore,
My work, also, will never end.

August 17

God's Love never comes
To an end. It just keeps
Growing and growing
And growing...
Encircling us in
Complete joy and safety,
Forever....

August 18

I will never be
Completely happy, until
I win God's Love.
I must be obedient to
His Laws and love
And respect everyone.
I move forward to victory,
Not giving up, until
God and I are one.

August 19

Do good; see good
Be good; hear good
Think good; live good.
This way I will attract
God's Undivided Attention.

August 20

Express heavenly
Love in your life
In all the things that you do.
Let that be your ultimate goal.
Then you will be
Able to really define "Happy".

August 21

I will express love in
All of my endeavors.
I will speak to others
In a soft and loving tone.
I will serve others
Lovingly and willingly.
Love never fails to
Bring a smile to all involved.

August 22

My positive and negative
Experiences will help
Me to grow.
They will
Help me to appreciate the
Lessons learned in a good
Or bad situation.
I will be taught
Valuable lessons from
These circumstances.

August 23

I will make the word Love
Number one in my
Vocabulary.
Because:
Love is God.
Love is Truth.
Love is Infinite.
Love is Joy.
Love connects all the dots
Making my world beautiful.

August 24

Look beyond the outward
Appearance of others…
The face; the clothes; the shoes; the hair.
Try to really see who is this person.
Get to know him, heart to heart;
You will see that you and him
Or her, are made of the same stuff…
God's stuff.

August 25

Don't worry that you don't
Know everything.
For no one does...
Stay open and receptive
To learning, no matter what age you are.
You will acquire some knowledge
And bits of wisdom every day.

August 26

Why should I seek
God early in life?
Because I am still young,
Energetic and without a lot
Of attachments, yet.
We, the youth, are the
Wealth of our country.
We can help to bring about
Great change that will
Uplift others by always
Keeping God first.

August 27

I will develop a loving relationship
With others, by looking beyond
Their imperfections, mistakes
And personalities.
I will strive to feel that
Soul-soul connection
Between us.
We can then become
God-connected.

August 28

When you own something,
You don't have to ask,
"Is this mine?"
When you have God's Love,
You don't have to ask,
"Where is God's Love?"
You will know that
God lives in your heart
And He is all yours.

August 29

God is my Magic:
I believe in myself;
I give generously;
I dream magnificently;
I live big-heartedly,
I love selflessly....

August 30

The secret is out!
God is Number One
In everyone's heart
And in every home, all
Over the world.
Spread the word!

August 31

When the serenity of a
Beautiful love song about God
Plays in my head, I feel it is for
My ears only.
I am still and surround
Myself in His sweet
Fragrant Love.

September

September 1

God sometimes speaks to me in
Harmonious musical notes;
Accompanied by celestial
Instruments that help calm me.
I feel He is letting me know
That I can talk to Him anywhere
And He will answer me
In ways that I will understand.

September 2

We have the power to control our mind
And take positive leaps and bounds
On our path to enlightenment.
Remember:
Meditate; be joyful and don't despair.
Live in determination and faith.
Be about victory!

September 3

Let's strive for harmony in the world,
Where every person is safe;
The color of your skin;
Religious differences;
Hair style or language
Should not matter.
It is time for us to
Make a Love connection.

September 4

Peace is a feeling that wraps itself
Around you, letting you know
That you are never alone.
The Heavenly host of angels
Daily surround you.
But more importantly,
The Lord of Peace
Never, ever leaves your side.

September 5

The way I feel in my heart,
Knowing that God lives there,
Is such an awesome feeling.
I share that feeling with others
By sharing my smile or a kind word.

September 6

I keep God in my heart.
That is His home within me.
It is a quiet sanctuary where I
Can go whenever I wish.
I talk with Him or just sit quietly.
This is Our sacred space.

September 7

I live in the now.
The present is
All that I have.
I live in the moment and
Do the best that I can.

September 8

Love yourself, unconditionally.
Acknowledge your flaws; we all have them.
However strive to replace bad
Flaws with good habits.
This can be accomplished over time
With lots of practice.

September 9

Peace is delicate but strong;
Delivering powerful testimonials of how to
Co-exist and surround ourselves in love
Without hurting anyone or anything.
Let's live in ease with peace of mind.
Let's do this.

September 10

When I eat ice cream, candy or cake,
The honeyed taste last a minute.
But, when I think of God,
The sweetness remains much longer.
I just need to concentrate more on God
So that loving feeling will
Last forever and a day

September 11

When you truly begin to
Feel the love of God within;
The love of God will just
Keep on growing,
Forever.
It will not go away.
Hence, God is in your house;
Deep within your heart of hearts;
Forever surrounding your
Temple in divine nectar.....

September 12

I will walk in God's Light,
Forever.
For His Light is majestic,
Healing and peaceful.
Encircling myself in His
Rhythms of esoteric sounds
And waves of infinite love,
I will always dwell in
God's Holy Light.

September 13

I become strong
Just by meditating
Upon You.
I become stronger,
Just by singing of Your glories.
I am my strongest,
When I put You first.

September 14

Lord:
You are my King of Kings,
With amazing and
Incredible power.
My perfect Love,
My true love whom
I can not be away from
For even a second.
For God and I
Are inseparable.

September 15

God, you are my World Cup;
My National Anthem;
My Fourth of July;
Where the excitement of
Firework explosions
Ring in my heart.
Touching my soul;
Overwhelming me
In shimmering streams
Of joy and pure bliss.

September 16

God is a Love song;
The perfect song;
Beautiful music swaying with
Pure Love in motion.
Living in God's
Kingdom of Light,
I am truly alive!

September 17

I am a divine expression
Of the great I Am.
I vow to do the right thing
To honor and respect all Creation,
With warmth and love.

September 18

Be happy!
Please the Lord.
Obey His laws
So you will not feel the
Pain of being ignored
By God.
It can feel like a thirsty person with
No water in sight, anywhere.
For obedience unto Him is the
Gateway to a flowing fountain
Of everlasting life with Him.

September 19

Sweet speech will bring
Peace to you
In all situations.
Soft and loving speech
Together, will endear
Others to you for life.
Be known for talking
Sweetly and peacefully.
Let this be your badge
Of recognition.

September 20

I will lay my foundation with love…
Build each wall with integrity…
Coat the roof with strength…
Paint each room with respect.
I will live in my home in comfort,
Knowing that I have Perfect protection.

September 21

I am not going to
Judge others anymore…
I am not going to
Disobey my elders anymore…
I am only going to
Live and be the best example
I can be for others
By walking my talk
Forever more.

September 22

I will speak lovingly…
I will give effortlessly…
I will share selflessly…
I will be about the
Business of Love.

September 23

Humbleness sets the
Stage for greatness.
I will strive to take the
Spotlight off of me.
I will dedicate my time to
Quietly serving others and
Not shout it from the roof tops.
Humbleness is
Next to Godliness.

September 24

Every day, I will strive to
Get closer to God.
I can feel His soft breath
On me as I take a walk, in
The form of a gentle breeze.
My heart fills with appreciation
And devotion.

September 25

Wherever I am right now,
God has placed me there,
To learn important lessons
That will help me grow.
I will always be grateful for His help
And guidance.

September 26

I have chosen to stay
In a place of love
And well-being,
Whether I am at home,
School, work, at church or at play.
This Love keeps me balanced and
In God's Territory.

September 27

I have the choice to
Choose whatever I want.
It is my wish; my decision.
I now choose to line up
My plan with what God
Has planned for me.

September 28

As I walk on this
Sacred ground called
Mother Earth, I feel
Her love expressed in
All of nature.
Her expressions of Love are
Like any mother;
Far-reaching, gentle
And forever....

September 29

In order to fix
My fears;
I must face them.
I will gain the victory!

September 30

Together, the essence of the
Family of humanity is
Warmth and closeness.
We are the ones
We have been waiting for.
Together we can
Change the world
For the better.

October

October 1

Motivation can come from within.
Inspiration may come from others.
Be enthused by people's success
On the road to God.
Keep your eye on the prize:
The Wonderful One: God

October 2

May I always dwell in your bright Light;
May I always walk in your guiding Light;
May I always feel the power of your mighty
Love, as I journey back home to You.
For You are my God;
My BFF:
Best Friend Forever.

October 3

Can I get a witness? Who else agrees
That God is good all the time?
God wraps His arms around me,
Keeping me safe and secure. He lets me know
That He loves me, and should have no fear.
Can I get a witness? All witnesses
Shout, "Amen!"

October 4

I just can't help but sing
Praises of You this morning.
May these joyful praises carry me
Throughout the day.
May the promise of Your Holy words
To deliver us from evil, be my chant today.
You are the Holy One…
My sacred Divinity…
Our Love is forever.

October 5

There is a light within me; in each of us,
That will never fade or go away.
This light is the extension of your
Omnipresence.
It lets me know that You are
Always accessible to me.

October 6

After sitting quietly, I pray that this
New day continues to bring me true
Joy and peace that only God can give.
I thank you, Lord, for
You are my everything;
My soft cloud of comfort and
A cream puff of divine sweetness.
Yes! I am yours, forever...

October 7

I will keep the serenity I receive from my
Morning meditation to help sustain me
Throughout the day.
It is a wonderful feeling
To be able to walk in bliss and peace
Upon sweet Mother Earth,
Thankfully acknowledging the Supreme One.

October 8

I rely on God for all of my needs.
He is continuously showering strength,
Fortitude and love upon me,
For me and through me.
Not only for me,
But for you, too.

October 9

Today I will rejoice and celebrate
This day that God has given.
I will spread joy by doing
Selfless service for others.

October 10

Today I wake up very happy.
I say my prayers and silently sit in meditation.
I am filled with joy and peace.
I am ready to start my day.

October 11

I am a child of God. I know it and feel it.
I love it. I carry this feeling with me
At all times. It is contagious and
Lovingly touches those
That I greet during the day.

October 12

Come rain or shine, I will
Be steadfast and strong as
An oak tree rooted in love in my pursuit
Of striving to live and be in peace
With my family.

October 13

One of the many gifts that God has given us is
choice. I make the choice to spread happiness
And joy. I choose to live in happiness and joy.
I pray that I will make positive choices
That reflects the pure heart of God.

October 14

Wherever you go today,
Give the gift of a smile to
Everyone you meet and greet.
Let others know that your
Unique smile is one of Your gifts to them,
Delivered from the infinite realms of
Happiness!

October 15

Be who you are always…
Let your good actions speak volumes of
What a wonderful person you are.
They will know where you are from.
Your address is of God.

October 16

Always let your light shine, so the depth
Of your devotion and dazzling aura
Can be an inspiration for others to follow.
Don't be afraid to take the lead.
Especially when you know the
True Leader is God.
Success will surely be yours.

October 17

Choose the path to God that fits you.
Then you can offer 100% of your love
And service back to the Cherished One.
He will shower amazing gifts upon you;
But to your astonishment!
You will look the other way
And only want His Love.

October 18

Follow your heart.
As long as you keep God first,
Then you will know that
You are doing the right thing
At all times.

October 19

Remember to wake up with a smile.
Meditate. Then prepare for the battle
Against the darkness that lurks within the
Mind. Put on your steel armor of fortitude.
Pray strongly to God to intercept when
Needed. Go! God is with you…

October 20

Stay true to yourself and God.
Then your life will be an offering
Unto the Most High, with the sweet
Smell of roses adorning
Your path of right action and wisdom.

October 21

I am beautiful because I
Learned to nurture and love myself.
Family, relatives and friends also played
A great part. I achieved this over time
And with the grace of God's
Loving guidance.
I am now able to love who
I see in the mirror.

October 22

Be clear about who you are.
Don't be afraid to look into
The mirror and see yourself;
Know yourself; honor yourself.
Love yourself and everything
About yourself.
Then you will
Be free and open to receiving
God's Love and Mercy.

October 23

Give yourself permission
To give yourself the
Green Light to live your
Life in peace, joy and in
Service to the Lord.

October 24

Do you feel the true
Essence of who you are?
Your life's purpose on Earth?
That is why silent sitting and
Prayers should be on your
"To Do List".
The answers lie inside of you.
Daily sit quietly with God
And your spiritual eye will open
To allow you to see or hear the answers
From the Lord who dwells within.

October 25

Breathe deep Yoga breaths.
Keep yourself balanced.
Inhale the fresh air of staying positive.
Now exhale the trials and tests of today.
Relax. Breathe. Be.

October 26

The most natural high in the world,
Is to be elevated by
God's infinite and blissful love.
Once you have experienced it,
You will naturally elevate yourself
To the great Realm of the
Highest Love of all.
You will never feel alone again.

October 27

I was liberated
When I realized that I was
Making correct choices because I
Felt and knew deep within that
It was the right thing to do.
No one had to tell me to do the right thing.
That is when I heard the freedom
Bell ring in my heart.

October 28

The worst disagreements
And battles are in the
Households; in the family.
Strive to keep your Light
Within glowing at all times.
Carry your bright sword of love and truth,
To help generate and maintain
Harmony within the family.

October 29

I am beautiful, so I smile.
God loves me, so I
Share my smile and my joy
With others.
It could be contagious.
Before I know it, peace and bliss
Will spread all over the planet!
Just because I smiled!

October 30

Get excited! Stay excited!
Be open for great
Opportunities in your life.
Stay positive and focused,
On what you truly
Want in your life,
And so it will be.

October 31

When a deep, spiritual question comes up
From within, I dig deep to find the answer.
God has given us a myriad of people and
Places to find answers to our questions.
But I wait and listen on the Lord to answer
My deep spiritual questions.
I am patient and wait
Only for His answer.
Through the power of meditation
The questions are answered.
I can now move forward.

November

November 1

Love conquers all.
I will strive to be about Love
Every second of the day.
I will make others happy and
I will bring joy to God. Now
That is an awesome feeling!

November 2

Combat fear,
Walk in confidence.
Exhale stress,
Inhale peace.
Breathe out hatred.
Embrace love.

November 3

Clap your hands;
Stomp your feet;
Snap your fingers;
Shake your head;
Wiggle your toes
And wave your arms.
Now shout,
"I love the Lord!"

November 4

I am so blessed to be
Able to think of God.
For when I do, a tsunami
Of love washes over me.
I am overcome in
Gratitude and love.

November 5

As the day draws to a close,
I have tried to stay in the same joyous
State of mind that I received during
My morning meditation. It is
Challenging, but very do-able.

November 6

God sent me into the world, with a
Clean body and pure spirit.
When my life's purpose is completed
On Mother Earth, I will return back
To Him, again, clean and with a pure spirit.

November 7

I value the laws of the Supreme.
I try very hard, everyday, to
Live them to the very best of my ability.
I know that one day, my determination
To live right, be strong and be fearless
Will enable me to be one with Him.

November 8

I cannot, nor can anyone that I know,
Turn our heads completely around to
Look behind us, like an owl.
But I do know that I can walk and
Look directly in front of me and
See where I am going to move
Forward in faith and trust.

November 9

I am about doing the work
For my Lord with an attitude
Of gratitude.
Despite the pitfalls and illusions,
I will stand firm in faith.
I will be a strong presence
And accomplish my purpose on Earth.

November 10

When I fall down, I don't stay down.
I get up, put on my imaginary boxing
Gloves that are filled with strength
And power. I will fight and destroy
The temptations that are holding
Me back from living a full life in God.

November 11

You are my Light; my Jewel;
My bright Diamond, that lights
Up my world.
You are…
I am…
One.

November 12

Dance to the true, inner rhythm of your soul.
Your soul that experiences no pain or death;
Bliss, peace and eternal life make up the soul.
This is the truth you should identify with;
Your eternal, happy soul.

November 13

Be around people who make you happy;
People who make you laugh and
Appreciate the beauty and joy of
Living a life of service and
Goodwill to others.

November 14

A happy person is a good person;
A good person is a loving person;
A loving person owes all of his
Happiness to God.

November 15

When that sweet feeling of love
Is swirling around in my
Heart and throughout my body,
It is the most delightful
Feeling in the world. I would
Dare say that the power of love is thrilling!
May we all be thrilled to the brim
With an over flow of adoration
For the Divine.

November 16

Wake up! Arise! Rejoice!
It's a brand new day.
I sit quietly to meditate;
Determined and motivated to
Receive God's mercy
Which will deliver me to
The feet of my Lord.

November 17

I am thankful to everyone
Who has helped me along the way
In this journey called life.
An attitude of gratitude with
Sincerity in my prayers,
Has instilled in me the strength
Of a spiritual warrior.
I refuse to look back.
This knowingness makes
My walk smoother.

November 18

All I need to be successful
And happy in my life, is to
Keep my thoughts on God.
Yes, it is challenging, but it
Is something that I strive for
Daily. I will never give up, no
Matter how many times I fall.
My goal is to see God,
Face-to-face one day.

November 19

There is an
Incredible gift that the
Lord selflessly gives to each of us.
It is cashmere soft;
It is coziness and love
All wrapped up in tranquility.
This unique gift that is so widely
Accepted and embraced by all
Is the sweet and priceless gift of:
SLEEP.

November 20

One day I made
The most amazing discovery!
Whenever I would point
My pointer finger at someone and accuse
Him or her of something,
I noticed that my thumb was pointing

Back at me! At the same time! Try it!
The lesson I learned was that since my thumb
Is pointing at me, I must look at myself to see
What part I too have played in this situation.

November 21

Whenever something doesn't
Feel right, I take notice. I just know it
Is not correct. God is sending me a message:
Take heed and listen.
I know that as long as I remain open,
My direct line to God will stay open.

November 22

I wake up feeling your love, God.
I meditate and await your command.
Guide me as to how I will be
Of service to you today. I am
Prepared and God-strong.

November 23

Peace comes through in
So many colors, shapes and
Sizes from people around the world;
Peace equals Quietness;
Quietness equals Happiness and
Happiness equals Contentment within.

November 24

When I allow peace to permeate
My life in all my thoughts,
My feelings and my actions;
I know that I am letting God take full
Control. I surrender. That is a grand feeling.

November 25

Before I do an activity,
I must ask God for His approval.
I will "feel" either a Yes or a No.
If there is the slightest unease,
God is telling me, "No".
I have faith that God is directing me
So, I will obey His advice.

November 26

I must take care of myself.
I must love myself, unconditionally.
I must stay strong, fearless
And responsible.
I must because I need
God's love in my life. Period.

November 27

I am grateful for good health.
I am grateful for a loving family.
I am grateful for Nature that
Surrounds me in beauty and awe;
That gently tells me that God is
Everywhere.

November 28

I am who I am! I see myself as
A beautiful, talented, caring, responsible
Extra-ordinary human being, living
An exemplar life on Mother Earth.
That's right, that's me.
Guess what?
That is also you.

November 29

There is Magic in the air.
That Magic is God…
The Supreme One in all of
His Glory, singing to us every day
In a language that each heart
Understands. I am so happy to be
In His Army to serve Him through
Serving others.

November 30

I kept asking God one morning while
Sitting quietly in meditation:
"Where are You? Where are You?"
I felt His response echo throughout my being:
"I am here. I reside within your heart."
I cried tears of joy, knowing that
God was and will always be with me.

December

December 1

When God doesn't respond to me,
I know that I have to be more
Dedicated to my spiritual work.
I have to get up early to Meditate;
Offer more service to others;
Love and honor others and myself,
Plus so much more.
I am not going to give up
Because having God's Love is
Priceless and magnificent.

December 2

I will develop the God-given
Powers within me, to keep going forward.
No matter what, in my quest for God,
I cannot and will not give up.
Never... Ever...

December 3

May I never lose sight
Of You, dear Lord....
May I always stay in perfect
Harmony with You, Sweet One...
May the day come when we will
Meet, face to face, and dance forever
In the sunlight of our Love.

December 4

I will maintain the attitude,
To offer the best service,
To the multitudes of people
Who are in need.
Give me the strength to do Thy Work.
Selflessly... Unconditionally.

December 5

Grow...
Stretch...
Move forward...
Create...
Introspect...
Live in joy with God.

December 6

I will live my life where
I will not forget You.
I will pray daily that my
Thoughts, words and actions
Are in sync with what
My God directs me to do.

December 7

Sitting and meditating quietly helps me
To focus on what I need to do.
It clearly helps me to see
My purpose and act accordingly.
I get lots of inspiration
And guidance when I tune
In to God on a daily basis.

December 8

I surrender my loud talking;
Talking-too-much and eating
Too-much-sugar self and all of the
Other unhealthy habits to God.
I need help, and I am not
Ashamed or afraid to ask
The Almighty for help.
Ask not, have not.

December 9

I now develop and embrace
All my good and productive
Habits that will lead me to
A good and righteous life.

December 10

Many roads lead to the Truth.
But there is only one God,
Who has many names:
God, Jesus, Jehovah,
Krishna, Allah, Muhammad;
Just to name a few.
Call the Lord in any language
And with a sincere heart
And He will come swiftly to you.

December 11

I want to get to the point
Of seeing God everywhere
And in everything.
Just think: the world would
Be the perfect place for all.
It would be Heaven on Earth.

December 12

I think of all my
Wonderful opportunities
To seek and discover
Who I truly am. I will
Achieve my goals through
Due diligence, patience and love.
All of my dreams will come true
Because I believe and have faith.

December 13

The source of our being
And of our happiness is
The one incredible God,
Who is with us always.
Through thick and thin, He
Never judges or scorns us. He
Is our dependable and loyal Friend.

December 14

I strive and I strive
And will keep striving;
Daily, minute by minute,
Hour by hour, to continue
To endeavor to conquer my fears
So I may achieve happiness
While living on Mother Earth.

December 15

As long as you
Are believers of the Lord,
Stay open to receiving His
Precious, all-encompassing Love.
His warm embrace will surround you
And guard you forever.

December 16

You are my Shepherd;
You are my Light;
You are my Super Hero;
You are my Shining Star.
You are my Everything
And All Things to me.

December 17

Making God number one
Has given my life greater
Meaning and direction.
You are my Interior Designer,
Fashioning me into full
God-Completeness.
Nothing will stop me from
Achieving my goals and dreams
As long as I keep You in
The forefront of my mind.

December 18

God, You are…
Therefore, I am…
Thank you, God, for
Breathing life into me
And allowing me to live fully
In love with You on sweet Mother Earth.
I am forever grateful to You.

December 19

I acknowledge the
Divinity within me.
The reflection of your Light shines
So very brightly around me.
Outwardly, I represent your Radiance.
I draw like-minded people to me.
I am blessed.

December 20

In the morning, I leave my
House fortified in God's Love,
To attend to my obligations:
Whether it's at work, school
or play. When I finish my duties,
I again place my attention on God.

December 21

As we move closer to the end of the year,
I still believe in myself and love myself.
I keep pushing forward;
Knowing that I am on the right
Path to the One who
Has captured my heart.

December 22

I love to feel the raindrops as
They fall gently upon my face.
Each drop feels soft and Heavenly
As they land on my cheeks, my nose, my
eyelids. I am in bliss as my Lord showers
Me with raindrops of Love.

December 23

We are one.
As soon as I forget that,
Please remind me, God.
When I forget, I don't feel so good.
When I do remember, it always feels like:
Thanksgiving;
Hanukkah;
Christmas Day and
Kwanzaa;
The joyous celebrations
All rolled up into one!

December 24

Let us celebrate the good in life and
Spread happiness wherever we go,
To the fullest extent.

December 25

The Three Wise Men encircled Baby Jesus and
Proclaimed His Sacred birth on Mother
Earth. Thus, a higher level of Truth and Self-
Awareness was introduced by Jesus, which
Would help to spread and enrich His Message
Of peace and love for all the
World to embrace.

December 26

Sing a joyful song loudly.
Let it reverberate within your heart,
Mind, and soul, continuously....
Then share your love song with others.

December 27

There are several ways to speak to the
Person who needs help and encouragement.
And it is the same way we should speak
To everyone: With love and compassion.

December 28

I will remember the many ways I adore the
Lord, whenever I speak gently and do selfless
Service. Every time I sing His Holy Names,
I will remember the many ways
I worship and praise the Most High.
I draw myself closer to living the
Good life with Him daily...

December 29

I will prove to God how much I love
Myself by the way I treat others.
I will treat them with love, kindness and
Understanding. The same way I want to be
Treated by others.

December 30

I will make each day more successful than
The day before, by moving closer to the Goal.
This way I receive more bliss;
Cultivate more devotion;
Live more joyously and
Dwell in happiness daily.
God is so very good to us.

December 31

As the old year comes to an end,
I am happy with how I lived.
I acknowledge all the mistakes
I have made and ask You for forgiveness.
As I step into the New Year, I am filled
With renewed strength, courage and faith.
I promise to stay strong and fight
The fight and walk the path, until
I meet My Maker, face to face, again....
HAPPY NEW YEAR...

I humbly offer all my love,
appreciation and praises to God.
I humbly offer my sincere gratitude and
adoration to my Spiritual teacher,
Swamini Turiyasangitananda.
Thank You Both for Everything…

ABOUT THE AUTHOR

Brahmashakti Fudail was born and raised in Mt. Vernon, New York. Her love for writing started at the age of 10 and her first poem was published at the age of 19. Mrs. Fudail is a retired elementary school teacher. She has been a student of meditation for over thirty years and follows an Eastern philosophy. Through meditation, prayers, self-introspection, reading spiritual and uplifting material and befriending dynamic people, she has been led to writing this book of inspirational thoughts for the young and the old. She is married with two grown sons and lives in southern California. This is her first book of inspirational thoughts written with both the young and old in mind. She is currently working on her next book.